This book is for

_____

MAY THIS BOOK HELP ENCGOURAGE
YOU TO KEEP GOING1
YOUR BEST IS YET TO COME!

Wishing you the best.

Toi

1

Printed in United States of America
ISBN 979-8-9888749-0-4 (Paperback)
First Printing

This book was written as I continue to go through my healing journey.

My journey to becoming the best version of me despite the traumas I have experienced.

This version is now Toi 2.0.

As I do my own self-reflective shadow work and look at my life daily, I've put together this book based on past encouragement notes to myself, research, and therapy.

My goal is for someone to read this book, and begin their own healing journey, so they may get to a point where they no longer suffer from their past, and no longer are anxious about their future, instead they learn to love where they are today!

Enjoy and be blessed.

My Amari
I Will Always Advocate For You!

proud
RUTISM
mom

What's The Encouragement For Today?

This is a question many of us seek daily.
Day after day every human being in this world is trying to remain encouraged to keep going and try to make it to the next day.

At some point in our lives, each of us will experience heartache, trauma, illness, depression, financial hardship, loneliness, relationship hurts, and death; and each one of us will handle these situations differently based on the experiences in our lives.

The fact that you are reading this right now means that you are here for a reason.

This book was created to provide you with emotional strength and help encourage you throughout your day.

Every day is different, so please read an outline that best fits your situation or close your eyes and open a page for a message daily.

You did not come across this book by coincidence.
You are choosing to not give up and start healing some of the traumas you may have experienced.

Remember, everyone comes from different backgrounds and has their own beliefs, and although "God" is referenced in this book, you can fit your belief where it resonates.

CONTENTS

What's The Encouragement For Today?   7

Positive Affirmations   12

What is Your Trauma?   14

Daily Affirmations   16

21 Days   17

Your Next Level   18

Attachments   20

How To Get Life Working Again   26

Staying Focused   28

Important Principles For a Positive Day   30

Setbacks   32

Better Than You Think   33

Experiencing Death   35

Let it Go!   37

Declare Favor   39

Discouraging News   40

GOALS   41

What's Your Declaration For Today?   42

The Truth 43

How to Thrive 47

On Time 48

In the Midst 49

Prayer Share 50

Stay Alert 51

Holding On 52

Trusting Yourself 53

I Tap Out! 54

When You Get A Call 55

Your Heart 56

Pray and Trust 58

Difficulty Trusting 60

Being Thankful 62

Watch Out 64

What's Perfect 66

New Things 68

The Perfect Shoe 69

Your Body and Stress 71

Your Thoughts 73

How Do You Move God? 75

Reality 77

Prayer Reminders 79

A God-Given Vision 80

Set Your Focus on God 82

Unleashing 84

Miracles In Marriage and Relationships 85

What Belongs To You 87

Punishment 88

Do Not Worry 89

Being Successful 90

Speaking Over Your Life 91

Shut Down Fear 92

Big Faith 93

Thank You God 94

Your Manifestation List 96

Your Personal Affirmation List 97

Your Thoughts 98

WHAT'S THE
Encouragement
FOR
Today?

Positive Affirmations

The purpose of positive affirmations is to help you overcome and change negative thinking patterns and replace them with positive thinking patterns.

It has been a scientific fact, that positive affirmations are similar to exercising. It increases the number of good hormones in the brain that make us feel good and improves our mental, physical, and emotional health.

Regular affirmation statements about yourself, repeatedly, will encourage your brain to take what you're saying as fact. When your brain truly believes you can do something, your actions will follow.

Use your imagination to create the things that you want in your life because you get what you think about. You get what you speak about. You get what you see.

For example, in a few minutes, take a deep breath, close your eyes, think of what it is you are wanting the most.
Think of what it would feel like if you had it.
What would you do? How does it make you feel?

(Take a few minutes and do this now)

That feeling is a feeling of gratitude. It is the feeling of when you have something already and are grateful for it.

That is the space in which you should operate. The more you recognize this feeling, the more you will have to be grateful for.

Every day is a new day to start the life that you want to live.

You might not change the situation, but you can change how you look at your situation.

What is Your Trauma?

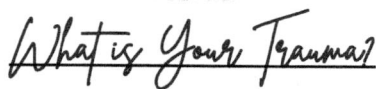

Many of us are dealing with past unhealed traumas on a daily basis and do not even realize it. Many of us have traumas that began as a child.

How do you know if you are dealing with trauma?

Trauma is when you experience an event in your life that was displeasing to you emotionally, mentally or physically. That event continues to exist and has an impact on your life later on.

Trauma is how you feel inside as a result of what happened to you. It is the emotion from the event that made you feel unwanted, not good enough, abandoned, or unlovable for example.

Trauma gets embedded into your brain as an emotional memory and then it is triggered when anything resembles it and shows up in your life.

In order for a person to be triggered, there must be something inside of them that is already unhealed. Their actions and their behaviors will always be the first clear indicator of it.

If you do not trust people or are easily hurt, it is your brain's natural reaction that shows that you were either possibly hurt a lot as a child, disappointed or betrayed.

Depression is a coping mechanism your brain has taught you to "depress", which means to push down your emotions.

When you have trauma, you simply develop coping mechanisms that your brain has taught you to survive.

Your brain will develop a method to operate in the reality that you create.

Once you acknowledge what happened to you, how it made you feel, and recognize that it is not happening to you right now, that is when you will begin your healing journey and God will continue to heal and shape you into the person you were always meant to be.

Daily Affirmations

It takes 21 days to make a habit.

Read the following positive affirmations daily and implement these things into your life to manage your life better.

Take a deep breath and read the following affirmations every day.

- ❖ I am loved and I love myself.
- ❖ I deserve to feel good.
- ❖ I look around and can find things that I am grateful for.
- ❖ I am happy, healthy and at peace.
- ❖ I am a money magnet.
- ❖ I am a good person despite any mistakes I have made.
- ❖ I deserve the best and I will receive the best.
- ❖ I have more coming in than going out.
- ❖ I am a great "mom/dad/grandmother/grandfather".
- ❖ I am free from all debt.
- ❖ I am grateful for all the blessings that are in my life.
- ❖ I am financially independent.
- ❖ Great things are always happening to me.
- ❖ I am open to receiving love.
- ❖ I am one with God and I am a vessel for God.
- ❖ I am wealthy and find it easy to make money.
- ❖ I am patient.
- ❖ The right people are in my life.
- ❖ I am whole. I have a destiny. I have a purpose.
- ❖ I have peace in my mind and joy in my heart.
- ❖ I make time for myself.
- ❖ I am strong.
- ❖ I have unlimited support.
- ❖ I have a perfect credit score.
- ❖ I live the lifestyle that I desire.

21 Days

God knows you by name. He knows your situation, the burden that you carry, and all that is on your plate.

You didn't ask for this nor did you plan for this, but God has always been there for you, even if it may seem as if he is far, he is not, he is near.

You may put on a face of courage in front of others, and behind closed doors you cry tears, but keep fighting!
Fight any depression, any worries, any illness, any insecurity, any self-doubt and keep giving your cares to God.

Remember, faith and fear cannot exist together!
You have to choose one.
His hands are always open for us!!

Mark each day to ensure you read these affirmations for 21 days!

DAY 1	DAY 2	DAY 3	DAY 4	DAY 5	DAY 6	DAY 7	DAY 8	DAY 9	DAY 10
DAY 11	DAY 12	DAY 13	DAY 14	DAY 15	DAY 16	DAY 17	DAY 18	DAY 19	DAY 20

DAY 21- change is happening!!

Your Next Level

The world we live in today is not the world we lived in years past. It is constantly changing, but similar obstacles will always remain. It doesn't matter how much money you have or what you look like.

The fact is all obstacles remain at all levels. Every person has an expiration date. So, it's a matter of what we are doing in the time frame that we've been given.

The area that you are fighting in the most right now, is not new to God. He has gotten many others through your situation. There are people around you that have gotten through and you are just waiting for your time to come.

While you are waiting, find the strength to be happy for those around you. Know that if they got through it, you are not far behind them.

God knows what you are missing in your life. He knows what you are needing right now. It is only when you shift your focus to what God has been telling you to do in your heart, that he will supply whatever you're lacking in.

He knows what bothers you. He also knows what you're capable of handling, but it's not until you learn whatever lesson you're supposed to learn, that you will be able to move to another level.

You will continue to repeat the level you are on until you have learned your lesson.

Everything is going to come when you focus on whatever God has put inside of you to do. Only you know what God wants you to do. He talks to YOU. You might think it is you talking to yourself, but it is not, it is your spirit connecting with God and God is telling you what to do.

You will feel your heart move when you're doing what you're supposed to do, and when that happens everything that you are lacking, money, stability, love, good health, will be given to you, because they all must be present in order for you to CONTINUE to do what it is God told you to do.

So that is why it is important for you to stay focused on God and all things will be supplied to carry out his plan.

Attachments

Children have a natural need to belong to their parents and be cared for by them. They cannot survive on their own until close to the age of six, because they must have love, closeness and be cared for by a person that is taking care of them.

God did not create us to survive without attachments to people.

We weren't designed to be alone or isolated. When you are alone, it intensifies the burdens of life that can lead to your brain creating unhealthy coping mechanisms and attachments in relationships. One form of punishment the government will do is place a person in solitary confinement, because human beings are designed to be together.

Based on whatever trauma you might have experienced in your life, will result through your behavior in your relationships.

This is especially true when a relationship is threatened, it will show what type of attachment style you actually have.

What Is Your Attachment Style?

There are four attachment styles in relationships.

- ❖ The first is a **secure** attachment style.
    - o When you have a secure attachment style, you are able to share your feelings openly.
    - o You're able to trust others and be trusted easily.
    - o You give love easily and aren't afraid of intimacy.
    - o You're not worried about a person leaving.

You are able to be independent, not needing validation, and won't get anxious when the person you're involved with doesn't text you back fast enough and feel as if they do not care about you or feel as if they will treat you like your last relationship did.

You have healed from your past traumas and no longer internalize a person's reaction to be a reflection of you.

Bit by bit we all can become fully secure in our lives. Instead of blaming yourself for your trauma, you have a choice daily to create your truth and stop replaying your past.

❖ The second is an **avoidant** attachment style.
- ○ This is when your relationship is great in the beginning, you get exactly what you want, then as time goes by you get bored and lose interest.
- ○ You become distant and subconsciously build a wall to avoid a person getting too close to you.
- ○ You dislike being put in a vulnerable space.
- ○ You avoid taking ownership of your actions and would rather change the subject to deflect from what is really going on with you.
- ○ You do not trust others.
- ○ You think highly of yourself, and are mostly a very high achiever, think you do not need anyone, you can take care of yourself, and are fine without anyone.

This attachment style is driven by trauma that has not been addressed and healed. It is likely that you have gotten hurt in your past, had a terrible breakup, were cheated on, that caused the lack of trust, and negative outlook of others.

This attachment style must do the work and look at yourself first and determine where did the first pain come from, and not internalize it.

Do not put the blame of the experience on yourself as if you caused it. It is an experience that happened to you and the result is the feelings you felt after the experience.

❖ The third is an **anxious** attachment style.
  o This attachment style does not like to be alone.
  o You find it extremely hard to be single.
  o You often need someone to provide you with reassurance that you are loved and that the person is not going to leave them.
  o You tend to be hard on yourself and easy on others.

This attachment style has a lot of communication conflicts in relationships because they are drawn to have more intense mood swings that demand a person's attention and feel the need to always want to fix their partner or care for them in some way. This can also be vice versa, where the person is wounded looking for a person to take care of them.

Nonetheless, it is an unhealthy attachment style that also requires reflecting and looking at yourself first to determine why and how are you reacting to other people's actions towards you.

You have to know that how a person treats you is not a reflection of you.

It is a reflection of what that person has experienced and encountered in their lives.

❖ The third is a **fearful** attachment style.
  o Individuals with this attachment style, simply put, view themselves negatively as well as the remainder of the world in a negative way.
  o They often think they are too broken or too wounded to be loved.
  o They often do not like themselves or others.
  o They do not trust others, so they hate opening up to people.

This attachment style usually thinks that all men or all women are bad, or all relationships have issues and would rather remain stuck in an unhealthy relationship, because they expect for the next one to be just as bad. So at least they know the demon that they currently have then another one.

This is a clear indicator of past unhealed trauma wounds and self-reflection is needed. Learning not to place blame on yourself but acknowledge and recognize where did this come from.
No human being is designed to be alone.
We need people to survive.

You are now in transition! Once you know something, you cannot un-know it.

Your transition begins when you can be truthful about your reality.

Look yourself in the mirror, admit your failures, admit your flaws, and what you did to contribute to where you are in life today.

Do not stay there.
Your past happened.
Your past is over.

You have the ability to change the way you respond to people when you know that what they are doing has nothing to do with you! It has to do with how they perceive themselves.

This is when you begin to move forward to begin healing yourself and allow God to step in and do things his way!

Release control.

How To Get Life Working Again

We all have times when we question ourselves and the decisions we've made in our lives. It's important to know what influences you when you're making decisions in your day-to-day life.

❖ Are you a person that makes decisions based on how you feel in the moment?

❖ Do you make decisions out of pressure, worrying about what others may think?

❖ Do you make decisions based on what you can get away with?

❖ Or do you make decisions based on your principles and morals?

It's important to be aware of how you make decisions because if you have experienced trauma, you can have a hard time with your emotions, such as, being angry, having anxiety, being sad, or shame and can cause you to either feel too much or feel too numb.

Let's get life working again! Take a deep breath! Count to 3 and exhale!

Write a letter to each person in your life that has deeply impacted your life and forgive them for how they made you feel.

Write a paragraph to your mom, your dad, your ex-spouse, your children's father, your children's mother, etc.

FORGIVE them of what they did to you and let them know how they made you feel.

Read it out loud, so your brain can hear it.

This is when you need people in your life who do not need anything from you, they will listen to you, agree, and have faith so you can keep pushing forward!

Sometimes God will let your condition get worse so that your faith can increase. God is faithful even when we're not.

Times can seem like it's working against you, but that's all it is, it is a "seem".

You must remember everything is working for your good!

Staying Focused

We must learn to seek out a relationship with God first and find out what it is he is wanting for our life.

Do not worry about tomorrow; tomorrow will worry about its own day.

Release your faith for what you are wanting today.
Make it your business to tell others how good God is.
Release your faith for what God has for you.

How do you do that?

❖ Confess and make an agreement regardless of your situation.

❖ Take action with your confession.

❖ Act out what you are asking for.

❖ Pray, make a request to God for what it is you want.

❖ Make a declaration, declare what you are wanting.

Remember, there is power inside of you! You can speak about God's goodness based on events that have happened in your life, where God has shown up in your life and provided a way when you thought there was no way.

Remember, the time when you didn't know how you were going to get through, but somehow, you made it!

If he did it then, he will do it again.

Important Principles For a Positive Day

The **FIRST** most important thing you must do for a positive day is:

Be aware of the words you are speaking today.

- ❖ Pay more attention and make a choice to speak more positively.

- ❖ Say what you want to happen today.

- ❖ Make the choice to say, "Today is going to be a good day".

- ❖ Do not say, "Here we go again, another miserable day".

- ❖ Make the change and speak what you want your reality to be.

The **SECOND** most important thing you can do for a positive day is:

Do Not take anything personal if it's out of your control.

Although easily said than done, you cannot control every part of your day. There are times when things are out of your control, but that does not mean it is your fault.

Do not take an outcome that isn't to your liking personally.

When you think this way, you create more stress on yourself and create negative outcomes in your day.

So today choose to release control.

The **THIRD** most important thing we can do for a positive day is:

Do Not make any assumptions:

When you make an assumption, you are setting yourself up for failure, because you are believing what you are feeling is to be true.

Assumptions only occur when there is a lack of communication.

So today, make a decision not to assume.

The **FOURTH** most important thing we can do for a positive day is:

Make an effort to do your best today.

When you set the intention to be aware of the things you say, to not internalize things, and to not assume, you are then trying your best to have a positive day.

You control where your energy goes.

Setbacks

Sometimes we go through times when we feel like we are going backwards. Just because you are having difficulties does not mean you are not in God's will. God is ordering your steps; he is ordering a setback. Just like there are seasons for growth there are seasons he have you go backwards.

God won't allow a setback if it is not going to work for your good. Whatever your setback is, God will send something better. Everything in your life that does not benefit you will be removed, so we can focus on the things that are moving us forward.

The only way to increase is to lose something. There are times in life where we will lose something that doesn't make sense. Recognize that without going backwards you won't have growth. God has new levels for you to see.

When things happen that don't make sense keep expecting God's favor and prove to God that you're faithful in this season.

Don't be discouraged, it is a sign that new is coming. Don't get bitter and complain. Remember, it is only a season and make the decision to trust God.

Better Than You Think

God is able to do far more than we can even ask, think or even dream of.

When we go through storms and challenges, we grow stronger when we wait on God.

If you allow God to do his work, you will be better off. Remember, this too will pass. We do not want to go through things, but it makes us who we are today.

God is with you. Just because you're going through things does not mean he doesn't love you.

God will give you the desires of your heart, but you have to step out on faith.

You can't stay in the same place and hope and pray that things are just going to happen. You have to do something, take action, and allow God to work through people and opportunities.

Don't be afraid of the storm or mountain that you see, walk through it.

You're going to get through it!

You are going to win! It is only a matter of time.

Just go through your storm the right way.

Get what you're supposed to get from your storm.

You will be wiser and stronger if you go through it the right way.

You might be going through it today, but it won't be long until you see the other side.

It is not an "IF", it is a "WHEN".

God says "WHEN" it happens.

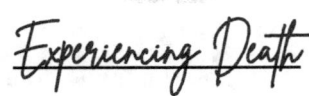

Experiencing Death

No matter how much we may want to try, we cannot stop death from occurring. Death is something we will all face at some time or another.

Losing someone you love can change your world and there is no right or wrong way to mourn.

God knows you will experience grief in this lifetime; however, you're not meant to go through it alone.

He wants you to seek comfort and rely on him and others to relieve you of your sadness, broken heart, and give you support.

Take every day one step at a time. What you're dealing with can feel overwhelming and make you feel like everything is out of control, but it's not, God is always in control.

To the natural eye, you simply can no longer physically see them, but that doesn't mean they are not there with you.

It doesn't mean their spirit doesn't continue to watch over you, help protect you, and send you signs that they are still with you.

You may sense they are near, by receiving chills all over your body, finding objects that have been lost, through electronics, finding dimes or pennies, seeing random lady bugs, butterflies and birds are all signs.

You're not crazy.

Try to find comfort knowing your loved one is near and is watching over you, but the biggest thing, know they are not far and are remembered warmly deep in your heart!

Let it Go!

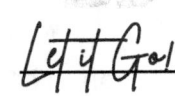

God wouldn't allow things that are not meant to happen, happen.

God will also remove people that are not meant to be in your life. You cannot embrace what God has for you if you are still holding on to the old. Old always hurts.

If you were supposed to have something or someone, it, or they, would still be with you.

Trust God when you don't understand. Just as God opens doors, he also closes doors. The best thing you can do is let it go and trust that God knows what he is doing.

When life isn't turning out how you are expecting it to go, you have to trust that he is still in control. Quit reliving the mistakes that you have made. Trust God with your successes and your failures.

Be at peace with what is behind you. Don't stay stuck in your past feeling sorry for yourself. Move forward.

Even if you do not understand it, God is working behind the scenes, and if God doesn't want you to have it, you simply will not have it.

If you don't let it go, you will stay stagnant.

You could be waiting for God to change things when God is waiting for your attitude and how you look at things to change.

Your outcome starts in your thinking.

You can't think the same way and expect things to change and have different results. Stay focused on what's puts in your heart.

There will always be people that may not like you for nothing you have done. It is you being you.

You need to let them go.
Let negative relationships go.

If someone does not add value to your life, let them go!

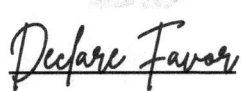

Declare Favor

Every day you should declare that favor is on you.
Declare it constantly.

Don't think discouraged, you have to speak these things out of
your mouth. Speak that favor is over your life. The more you
thank God, the more you are going to see favor in your life.

Release your faith and say, "Thank you God that favor is on my
household causing us to be abundant." "Thank you, God that
favor is keeping the wrong people from defeating me and I am
able to overcome obstacles everyday".

❖ The favor of God opens doors that you can't open.
❖ The favor of God brings healing.
❖ The favor of God brings favor over your finances.
❖ The favor of God causes you to stand out.

The dreams that God puts into your heart, you must speak
favor over them. When God gives you a dream, he will give
you everything that you need.

He will cause it all to come together for you.
It will not take long to get your dream once you have favor!

Discouraging News

You might've just received some discouraging news, but you have to know and remember that people do not control your destiny.

No matter what the situation may be! People do not have the final say. People do not know what God can do in your life.

Don't let them talk you out of your dreams.
Do not let them convince you of what you're capable of doing.
All it takes is one touch of God to move you ahead.

They may be negative, discouraging, or condescending, but let it go in one ear and out of the other. None of that can stop your purpose and you will beat the odds.

He didn't bring you this far to leave you where you are.
He didn't let you go through all of this to leave you stuck.
So Keep going. Don't get discouraged.

God has people lined up that will be behind your dreams. You won't have to convince them, they will be for you, even if they don't want to. You will be surprised at who God will use to help you get to your destiny.
So, keep going!

GOALS

When setting goals try not to set too many at one time.

Whether it's learning to be more disciplined with your finances, disciplined in refraining from certain foods, or disciplined in relationships.

Setting goals is important to keep you aligned and motivates you to get to a higher level in life.

Every time you set a goal, it's important to invite God into what you are trying to accomplish because he will answer you when you call on him and help you reach your goal.

He will use challenges to stop you from doing things that are destructive to you or will encourage you to do what is right.

We all have a purpose to fulfill here on earth. When you set a goal, you are letting God know you are wanting to do well with the life that has been given to you.

Setting goals is showing God you believe his word to be true. He will provide you with the right goals to set, gain clear direction, focus, increase productivity, and stay motivated to achieve them.

All you must do is ask!

What's Your Declaration For Today?

Don't keep talking about the problem.

At your lowest moment God is going to show you who he is. It may seem impossible, but instead of talking about what bothers you, talk about how you know God is going to fix your problem. That despite what it looks like, God has a solution.

When people don't treat you right, don't get bitter or angry, just know that something great is on the way.

Declare greatness every morning!!

❖ I declare the favor of God is on my life. I declare favor over my family, over my child, over my finances, favor while at work, and favor with my business.

❖ I declare that favor is causing the right people to come into my life.

❖ I declare I am free from sickness, pain, depression, addiction, and heartache.

❖ I declare and speak favor over everything that is trying to stop me.

❖ "I declare things are going to happen sooner than I think, and I will reach the fullness of my destiny!"

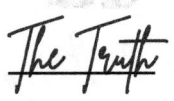

The Truth

Truth is needed even if it hurts.

The truth can hit you to the bottom of your soul that you physically feel it in your heart and in your stomach.

However, no matter how the truth may make you feel, you cannot grow if you cannot accept the truth.

❖ It could be the truth that the relationship you are in is unhealthy and you're choosing to pretend that the relationship is great, instead of accepting your reality and seeing your partner for who they are and how they make you feel.

When you pretend, you are creating a false reality in your head. No matter what you want or do not want, your reality is your reality, and your reality cannot improve if you do not accept your truth.

❖ It could be the truth that you noticed your parents haven't been getting along, but in your mind, you choose to pretend instead of accepting reality, forcing two people to remain together and pretend that they are happy and now the entire family is trapped in this false reality of pretending, when in actuality they are miserable and would do a better job co-parenting and living in their truth.

Remember, where there is truth, there is peace.

❖ Truth could mean admitting you like your same sex and being happy finding a fulfilling relationship, instead of trying to pretend that you do not and force yourself into a relationship with someone that you're not even attracted to.

It is always better to admit you are incompatible with someone within 30-days of dating versus admitting that you are not compatible after you've been married with kids for 5 years. You could've avoided years of suffering and pain and impacting each others lives.

❖ It could be the truth of telling someone that there is a possibility a child may not be theirs, versus to pretending and creating a false reality and them finding out years later. The impact will be even more severe and devastating than finding out initially.

It is always better to admit the truth when it is small versus to avoiding, making a situation much worse.

❖ It could be the truth of something so simple as you painting a wall and falling off of a latter, breaking your leg, and instead of admitting something doesn't feel right and go to the hospital, you decide to walk on it and pretend that it doesn't hurt, only for it to later swell, turn colors, and you become in unbearable pain.

If you do not look at the truth of your reality you cannot solve your problem.

❖ It could be the truth of admitting your family is dysfunctional, competitive, unsupportive, full of envy and jealousy between siblings as they each fight for love and approval from the parents, even as they are well of age, they still yearn for the love and approval of their parents. Meanwhile, the children aren't even aware that the love they are fighting to receive, the parents do not know how to give, as they themselves were not shown or did not receive healthy love and now this family has generations that are stuck in a vicious unhealthy cycle.

When families remain in trauma and remain in a false reality of normalcy, because this is how things have always been done, or how someone has always behaved, it stops the family from growing and healing and allowing everyone to speak their truths.

When a family is able to speak their truths, it causes the family to build closer bonds and heal, as you may not be aware that a family member feels a certain way and can help heal a trauma in their reality.

At some point everyone will face the reality of their truths in life.

Finding out the truth and accepting the truth only leads you to have a successful outcome no matter how it makes you feel.

When you make decisions based on truth you will have a long and successful outcome vs a short-term result from when you are always pretending and living in what you want things to be instead of what they are.

Truth will always be revealed eventually.

A person has to want to see the truth.
You cannot make them see it.

No change can happen if you are pretending.

Only truth will cause you to heal and change your reality.

Accept your truth and start living in your reality today for a better tomorrow!

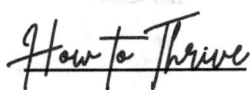

How to Thrive

Give God your regrets from your past.
Even if it is a mess. God loves you so remember that he intended for you to flourish. So, call on God to do these things for you.

How you think is how you will be. You are what you think.
Thrive on being healthy. Stay active and enjoy life.

If you neglect to expect God to do something for you, then you won't see it. You must have expectations.
Do not let negativity move you out of who you are.

Speak good about what you do have.
Where you are right now.

- ❖ Stop speaking bad about your situation.
- ❖ Stop putting limits on what God can do.
- ❖ Stop giving the devil credit in every situation.

Do not live your life by your feelings.
It is easy to feel like you're alone, but God is with you.

Recreate your spirit. Change your thinking.
Do not let your emotions or life pull you away from the promises that God has for you. Remember you will have what you say and God wants you to thrive not just survive!

On Time

God's timing is always on time.
Do not get stuck on how you used to be.

Watch who you associate with and do things to renew your mind daily. This will produce real success.

The favor of God can get you into places money can't get you into.

God desires for you to seek him.
You do not have to live a life reliving your past decisions, in regret. You will live a joyous life.

If your mindset doesn't change, nothing in your life will change. You must change your mindset; change how you think and you will begin to have the life that you want.

Everything that the enemy has, God has the opposite.
Where there is rain, there is also sun.
Where there is Hell there is also Heaven.

All of your needs will be supplied once you shift your thought process.

In the Midst

God chooses you. You did not choose him.
He acknowledges you.

God has chosen you for a specific task to perform on his behalf. It doesn't matter about your past. Your past is part of your purpose.

In the midst of your storm, God will come and show up in your life to let you know he is not gone. He is right there with you.

In the midst of your storm, keep your heart right. Let God fight your battle. He will save those who love him and will protect those who acknowledge him.

In the midst of your storm, acknowledge God. In many cases your storm is not about you. He will use your life so others will have the chance to see how he operates. This will cause for others to want to build their own relationship with him based on what they've seen happen in your life.

Everything is a matter of perspective of how you see things.
So stay humble, and try not to do thing your way.
Do not miss what God has really planned for your life.
Acknowledge God, it means everything to him.
Acknowledge Him and He will ALWAYS acknowledge you!

Prayer Share

Heavenly Father, I start today thanking you for your presence in my life.

You are a God of healing and a God of restoring and I thank you for life today. I thank you for the ability to breathe, see, and hear. I pray for your Mercy, your Grace, and your perfect Peace over every area of my life.

I pray for forgiveness for everything I have done and said that was not pleasing to you. I pray that you help me to heal and become a better version of myself.

I pray that you continue to comfort me when I am weary, guide me when I am confused, and lift my spirits when I am tired. Continue to bless me so I may be a blessing to others and keep me protected from danger or anyone seeking to do me harm.

I pray for my family and friends, that they are healed, blessed and develop a relationship with you. That if they are hurting, lost, or misunderstood right now, that they know you can hear our hearts even when we do not know the words to say.
I know that you know what is best for my life and as long as you are in it, I will have the best outcome.
I call upon you to show out in my life. Thank You, Amen.

Stay Alert

Guard your heart. The enemy may use the closest people to you to harm you, but remember, God is in the forefront of your life.

Despite what your situation might look like, look for opportunities to move forward.

There are going to be challenging and difficult times, but God will provide you with peace.

Fear and anxiety will not overtake you!

Be confident and know God hears you EVERYTIME you pray.

Think about a time when you did not know how you were going to get out of a situation, but somehow you did.
That somehow was not you. It was God.

So, if he did it then, then you know that the answer to your prayers is on its way.

It's not an, IF, it's a, *WHEN*!

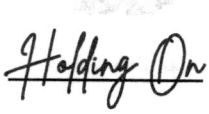

Holding On

Hold on to the vision that God has given you.
Keep the vision of God at the front of your mind.

Hold on to what God says.
Hold on to the promises of God.

Learn to slow down and learn from your experiences, so that you can move to your next level in life.

If you have an area in your life that you are struggling with, lay it out before God in detail and watch how it will come true. Amazing things will begin to happen in your life.

Recognize that every good gift comes from God.
Release the control of your life and hand it over to him.

Do not depend on your own resources.
When you give God control, he will bring change.
You won't see things the same.

Say, "God grant me the strength to accept the things I cannot change," and watch how quickly you will be like a palm tree, beautiful but not easily broken, able to bend at any storm that may come your way!!!

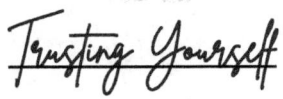

Trusting Yourself

Do not do things your way. You can't trust yourself.

When you do things your way, you will lose focus.
God has to help you every day if you're going to have a successful life.

When something bothers you, you need to take it and place it before God.

- ❖ Attacks
- ❖ Financial Hardships
- ❖ Sicknesses and Diseases
- ❖ Your Job
- ❖ Your Temper
- ❖ Your Anxiety,
- ❖ Things that are out of your control

Place them all before God. Nothing is too hard for God.
Do not continue to do things your way.

You must remember that God will never leave you nor forsake you.

You may feel like you are left alone but you are not alone.

 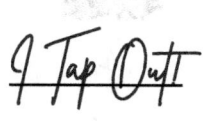

I Tap Out

Do not tap out.
God is with you. God has you in a special place.

When you tap out, you miss the opportunity to grow. If we find ourselves lacking, it is because you have moved away from God. There is a void, an emptiness that only God can fill.

If you put things or people before God, it will not work.
You must learn to listen to what God wants you to do.

When we tap out, we miss our connection.
Things that are essential to our success and where God is wanting us to be in life.

Be careful of burning relationships.
You do not know the blessing that can come through relationships.

Get the right people in your life.
Just because someone does not agree with you, does not mean they are not for you.

Find a support group. Do not be ashamed.
You never know who you could be a blessing to.

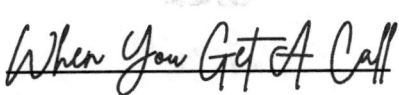

When You Get A Call

When God shows up it's not always convenient. God has great plans so you must be willing to be inconvenienced in your life.

What has God been calling you to do to reach lives that you have not been responding to?

Every one of us has a special gift, a talent that can be used to help others in some way.

There are several ways that you need to respond to God's call.

Respond with your head. Hear his voice and get understanding to know what God wants you to do.

Before God can get to your heart he must get in your mind. The battle takes place in your mind. Many blockages that you have are in your mind.

Meditate and train your mind. If you do this, you will prosper and will always find success. God will keep you in perfect peace if your mind stays on him.

Don't just sit around and do nothing. Remember faith without work is dead.

Your Heart

Your heart is your spirit. It is the internal part of you.

For example, if you believe in your heart, you will have it. Your heart will then determine your ability to move forward so that you can receive it.

The heart is so powerful it can disrupt everything in your life and even affect you physically.

Having a broken heart can affect you mentally.
When the heart hurts or is troubled, it really affects your mind.

When the head and the heart are on one accord, they become powerful in the life of the person.

It can be seen in the subconscious and conscious mind.

The conscious mind operates only at a 5% level.
The subconscious mind handles everything else.

There is a link between the subconscious mind and the heart.

Your subconscious mind speaks to you in dreams. God will talk to you through dreams and visions.

Whatever is sown in your heart, that is what will grow.

The subconscious mind operates on a whole different level.

You have to feed it.

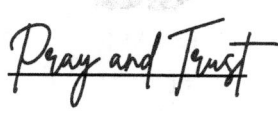

Pray and Trust

Pray and trust God with your situation.

- ❖ Your life.
- ❖ Your health.
- ❖ Your children.
- ❖ Your finances.
- ❖ Your career.
- ❖ Your heart.

Whatever is bothering you, trust God with it.

Sometimes you're dealing with issues that you're not supposed to because you're not handing things over to God.

How often do you seek God?
Introduce God to your situation.

Believe God is the answer to your situation.
Do not concentrate on the problem, just say "Situation, meet God... God, meet my situation" As silly as that may sound, sometimes you need to be just that literal with what you are going through.

Release your faith.
How do you do this? By the words that come out of your mouth followed by your actions.

What have you said about your situation lately?
What is coming out of your mouth?
What are you releasing your faith for?
All you have to do is simply believe that all things are possible.

Take authority over what is stressing you, over any anxiety.

Speak God into every situation that you have going on.

Everything starts with the words that come out of your mouth.

God will respond and provide you with answers.

He will not give you a life that you do not need him, at some point you will have no choice but realize you need God!

Difficulty Trusting

If you are having difficulty trusting God, just know that trusting God does not take time.

It requires a decision. You must choose to trust God when you're hurting even when you do not know what to do.

Everyone makes a decision off of trust.
Trust only takes time with a person.

How do you learn to trust God?

❖ Through personal testimonies.

❖ Listening to what others have gone through that caused them to believe in God.

❖ Remembering your own personal experiences that you have overcome. Thinking back to when God came to your aid and answered your prayers.

Hold on to it and recall it back to your mind when you are feeling doubtful. He is the same God back then and he is the same God today.

Learn to trust in God by telling others how good he has been to you.

Trust is built when you can feel when God is around you.

When you hear his voice and you keep moving forward.

Having trust in God will save you from unnecessary situations, attacks, heartaches, setbacks, and pains.

It even allows doors to open that were once closed.

God will come through for you.

Make a decision to trust God today.

Being Thankful

God is deeply concerned about you. He will make all things work together for the best outcome for your life.

Certain things are just common to life, that's unavoidable.

In this world you will have trouble. You will have challenging and difficult situations. But no matter what, give thanks.

Be thankful in good situations. Be thankful in bad situations.

Things are going to happen. But know you are going to win! You will have success.

Continue to say that you are blessed.
What you say out of your mouth is very important.

Do not speak negatively about your situation.
Only God knows if your situation can be turned around.

Do not focus on complaining about bills, about money, about love, about situations that are out of your control.

Yes, they exist, but you cannot quit or give up and stop believing.

Speak to your situation over and over and listen to your spirit.

Say whatever God tells you to say to turn your situation around and you will overcome your situation.

This is just a part of your journey.

❖ Ask God to give you wisdom that you didn't have before.

❖ Ask God to give you another level of strength that you didn't have before.

It is your faith that overcomes the attack, depression, and what aches your heart the most.

All things are possible to those that believe.

Don't quit. Don't stop. Don't give up.

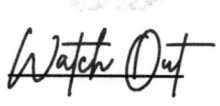

Watch Out

Watch out for distractions.
The enemy will come in and get you off your course from what God put on your heart and pull you away from what he has instructed you to do.

God is not going to give you instruction and not help you to do it. He will empower you and give you the strength to do what he wants you to do.

If you do not think right, you can't live right.
Your spirit helps you to think right. If you listen to your spirit, it will help you navigate through your life.

When you are in alignment with listening to your spirit, then you will be able to manifest the things you want in your life.

You can speak it. Listen. Claim it. Accept it.

Ask and you shall receive. Ask for wisdom.
God has the right person, job, career, healing all set aside specifically for you.

It might seem like time is running out, but God will renew the time if you focus on him.

Be still and let your spirit talk to you.

Set aside time to hear from him and speak to you.

Watch out for those around you that are envious of you, that speak negative, that make excuses, that doubt.

Receive what God is saying to you. He speaks to YOUR spirit, not theirs.

Do not be so easy to quit.

God knows the quickest way for what you are supposed to be doing.

Just ask and your spirit will show you.

What's Perfect

Sometimes you have to go through situations that are negative, but in that situation, there is a special blessing.

There is something great about it that causes you to go higher despite what it may look like.

There are several things you must do.
You must change your perspective and look at things differently.

Make up your mind that you are going to trust what God is saying.

Know that he can make every situation work out better than you can imagine.

Sometimes your situation can become your purpose.
Purpose is given when you are going through your hardest trial.

Do not count yourself out because of your past or any areas you may be lacking in.

God can still and will still use you. Everyone has weaknesses and downfalls. No one is perfect.

God knows your end. He knows what you need today.

Stop being afraid, stop being sad.

You cannot stay broken. Others are watching how you handle your situation.

God always has more than you in mind.
God always wants others to come to him. God wants to bless you openly so that others can see his glory.

So what is perfect? Absolutely nothing is perfect!

You will have ups, you will have downs, but wherever you are, God is right there with you!

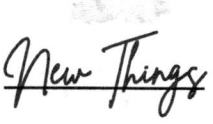

New Things

When you get ready to step into a new season you must let things and people go.

You cannot allow people or situations to keep you down and feel like you do not deserve it.

Sometimes things will go slow because God wants you to get something from it.

You might miss your blessing if you are holding on to something you were supposed to let go of.

Opportunity is always disguised because it looks like it is work.

Take control of yourself. Whatever is not right with God you have to release it.

Do not allow your thoughts to take control of you.
Remember thoughts become words, words become actions, actions become habits, and habits become a lifestyle.

When God tells you something you must believe it and have faith. Change your surroundings and watch what is coming out of your mouth if you're wanting to receive new things in your life.

The Perfect Shoe

Many of us like shoes. Some more than others.
Imagine walking past a shoe store and as you are passing by, a shoe on display catches your eye.

You instantly stop in your tracks because this shoe that is on display is the perfect style of shoe that you like, an exclusive color that does not exist anywhere you've ever seen, and the price is exactly right, however, you can't tell if it's your size or not.

Some of us are experienced enough to tell if a shoe can fit us or not, others must try the shoe on to see if it's a good fit.

Knowing this shoe is the right style, the right color, the right price, and overall looks fantastic, it's important to accept how the shoe fits.

Is it too small?
Are you going to try to stretch it and force it to fit?

Is it too big?
Are you going to act like it fits and try to fill it with fillers?
Knowing it won't stay on with just you?

It doesn't mean there is anything wrong with the shoe.

It is a perfect shoe.

It's just not the perfect shoe for you.

Don't try to make things fit into your life that God did not intend to be in your life.

That is you trying to do things on your own, how you want to do things, and not how God intended for your life.

God knows what is best for your life.
Stop trying to control everything!

If you take your hands off the steering wheel and depend on God to be the driver in your life, he will deliver what best fits into your life.

It will be a comfortable fit designed specifically just for you.

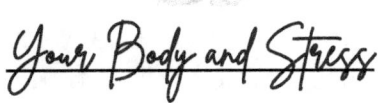

Your Body and Stress

Stress! Ohhhh Stress!
Stress is simply our natural body's response when we are experiencing difficult situations in our lives and are trying to control things ourselves.

When you are stressed, you might feel overwhelmed, or in constant thought trying to come up with solutions.
You may feel impatient, irritable, or even angry at times.

Stress is very much real in the body and can increase your risk for a stroke, heart attack, and hypertension.

Everyone will experience stress to some degree, but its only when you learn to relinquish control and hand what you are dealing with most in your life over to God and know that the situation was never yours to handle in the first place.

You have to come to a point where you trust God to not miss manage your life.

Trust God. Trust what he says.

There are times that your body isn't going to agree with your spirit. However, it doesn't matter because when your spirit receives a word from God, your body has no choice but to line up with what your spirit says.

If your body is sick and your spirit is well, then your body has to line up with your spirit.

Every word has power.
Do not trust God with your brain but trust God with your heart.

Watch your thoughts.
The way you think affects your body.

Your body is tied to your brain.
Remember the saying, "whatever a man thinks, so is he."

Every situation is an opportunity for God to be amazing in your life.

So, if you are stressed that means God isn't close, you do not have peace, and right now is the perfect time to give your entire situation to him and release control!

Right now say, "Lord, I hand it over to you, for you know what I need in my life, Lord I trust you!"

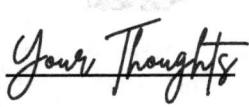

Your Thoughts

You are a spiritual being in human form, so you have to be mindful of your thoughts and stop any negative thinking.

The thoughts you believe will determine the reality in your life. Whether it is good or bad. What you believe will become your reality.

Stop thinking about your past.
Thoughts of your past only lead you to depression.

Stop thinking about your future.
Thoughts of your future only lead you to anxiety.

Accept what is going on in your life today.
Be grateful for today.
When you are grateful you become more aligned in where you are destined to be.
When you are grateful you become happier with yourself.

Choose to think about everything you are grateful for.
This puts you into a positive energy.

When you think about one thing that is positive, another one will come to your mind, and another one, and that is how you fill yourself with positive energy and control your thoughts from being negative.

Sit down, be still, calm your mind.

God is always speaking to you through:

- ❖ Visions while you are awake
- ❖ Dreams when you are sleep
- ❖ Sounds
- ❖ Voices in our heads

God's voice will sound like your voice when he speaks to you.

You must learn to listen.

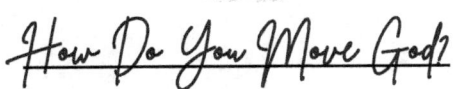

How Do You Move God?

Remember, it is the cry not the complaint that gets God's attention. Stop telling people your problems and talk to God about your problems.

God remembers what he has promised you. It is what he has put inside of you that you can't let go of. He knows the relationship that he has with you.

Remember it's about the connection and not the capacity that you have with him. God knows what you need better than you.

Once you pray to God for something, begin to thank him. You don't have to keep praying for the same thing.

Sometimes you need to sit back and think about all that God has brought you through.

Know that you are really blessed, because things can always be worse.

What has affected your life the hardest gave you what you're striving for today. If a problem didn't exist it wouldn't need you. God places you places not only for yourself but for others. Realize your gifts. You would not know your talents if you did not experience hardship.

You might can't see it, but God does things in our life that we can't see.

God will use you. What you are going through may not even have anything to do with you. It is about them, and he is using you to get to them!

Remember, God is watching and if you do good unto others God will do good to you.

Reality

God knows the things that you need before you even ask for them.

Prayer changes everything and everything changes with prayer. Your emotions, mindset, and situations.

Do not run from problems and confrontations. Confront all situations head-on with God. What you believe is important to what you are manifesting in your life.

God gives you free will, so you have to make a choice and call on God to enter into your life and your situation.

Whatever is going on around you in life should not affect you. God will help you in areas that you are struggling with.

Remember, God heals the brokenhearted and heal up their wounds. So, allow God to touch where you're hurting.

Take what is truly hurting you to God. He will touch your past and restore you.

To go to the next level in life, will require prayer.

When you start praying God starts touching the hearts of other people that can bless you.

Reality changes in prayer first. Your breakthrough will happen at the moment you believe God will do what you have asked him to do.

Remember nobody can keep what belongs to you!

Prayer Reminders

Don't worry. Just pray.

What you are supposed to be doing you cannot do without God.

Important Reminders About Prayer:

- ❖ Prayer will make you dependent on God. It allows God to know that you need him.

- ❖ Prayer will show your faith in God. God hears you and he will answer you, but you must talk to him first.

- ❖ Prayer will remove pride and ego. You are only great because God is in you. If God is not in you, you are nothing.

- ❖ Prayer will prepare you for greatness. Wisdom comes in prayer. Healing comes in prayer. Once you pray, take a step, and walk in faith.

Things will not remain the same when you pray.

A God-Given Vision

When a vision is from God it is something that God has said to you already.

Your vision should come from God.
The universe also responds to the word of God.
Do not say "I feel" or say, "I think".
Instead, say "God said", "God said".

God said write the vision and make it plain on tablets.
The vision is yet for an appointed time.

Don't get stuck looking at where you are but look at where you will be. Look at your vision.

Vision will give you a push through where you are.
Your words will change your situation.

In your vision you must know that if you see it, then you can have it. See yourself with what you want, and you can have it.

What do you see yourself with?

A new house, a marriage, traveling, a happy relationship, your children flourishing, increase in your bank accounts, your own business?

Whatever it may be, if you see God's vision then carry it out!

If you seek out God, God will give it to you.

God will and even use who you least expect to prosper you.

Set Your Focus on God

We cannot be successful, prosperous, or enjoy victory without God.

Seeing has nothing to do with physical things as spiritual things. When you open your spiritual eye, you will see a person for who they really are.

That's why you've heard, "walk by faith not by sight".
You must use your spiritual eye and listen to your intuition.

You must remember that angels are assigned to you.
Know what you have. There are always angels that are around you.

God is not concerned with whatever title you may have, but that you want to obey him.

Whatever God does for one person he must do for another. You can't accomplish what God has for you until you can see that God is in it.

You have to use your spiritual eyes. God will show up for every person that believes in him and relies on him. There is no limit to what God can do.

A blessing is an agreement that is aligned with God.
Watch what you say. You can curse your circumstances with what you say.

Regardless of what it looks like, you have look past the situation and bless your situation.

Learn to say thank you God, that I have everything that I need.

Do not think it takes time, know it only takes God!

Unleashing

God has times for you that have been set. You must know you are powerful and that the enemy is trying to make you think that you are weak. It is not the other way around. Not that you are weak trying to become powerful. You have to know that God has provided you with what you need to get through your trials.

You must draw back and remember all the times that God has got you through difficult moments in your past. The minute things are going well, the enemy will always appear.

God will give you what you've been asking for and the enemy will always appear to attack it. You must acknowledge God.

You are where you are based on the decisions that you have made in your life. Do not blame God. When you have power, you can take authority over your situation. If you're in emotional pain, you ask God to remove your pain. There can never be any success without any pain. Pain is a good situation. He's trying to get something through you so that you can get to your promise.

God will make you be in pain to bring something good out of you. He has a purpose for you. Your uniqueness is what is going to bless you.

Miracles In Marriage and Relationships

God cares about all relationships, particularly marriage. Your situation may look like he does not care, but he cares about all relationships.

There will be times of joy lost in a relationship, and this happens due to, not being ready, not being prepared for a marriage, a relationship, being untruthful, or not creating a safe space for each other to communicate effectively.

God must be invited into your marriage. You must have someone that knows God and can pray for your relationship. Do not give up. You must have faith. Fight with faith. The enemy will not want to let go, but you must know that he will.

When joy is running low in your relationship, you should:

❖ Assess yourself first and look at your attitude and how you are playing a part in the situation.

❖ Take a step back and look at your actions. The other person might've been wrong, however, ask yourself if you could've handled yourself better.

❖ Are your reactions coming from past traumas that you have not healed from.

❖ Did you allow negative things to come out of your mouth.

❖ Most importantly pray. Be quick to pray. Go talk to God when you see things are not right.

The moment that you start to pray is when the fight to your battle begins.

God begins to change things the moment that you start praying. You might pray for a long time and not see anything in the natural, but it's because it has to happen behind the scenes first to reach what you can see.

Even when you cannot see it, you must know that God is working on it.

The moment he heard your prayer, he put your miracle into motion.

What Belongs To You

People that keep praying, are the ones that have the most breakthroughs and promises fulfilled, so keep praying!

What belongs to you will come to you at the exact right time. What has your name on it, is heading your way.
You may think it's taking too long, but God doesn't change his mind. God has blessings stored up for you, you have to believe and do your part.

What God brings to you, will not be exactly what you thought or how it was to happen, but it will exceed your expectations, if you allow God to bring it to you.

What God has in store will be bigger than what you thought. There are a lot of things that are heading your way that has your name on it. You won't have to look for it. It will come to you.

While you are waiting for your promise, keep praying, keep believing, and staying in faith.

Don't get discouraged. Keep praising God for what you are believing for.

It will definitely come to pass!

Punishment

God does not punish you to teach you anything.
He tries to prevent you from your actions, so you don't have to go through the consequences.

God knows your mistakes but will bless you anyway.
How would you feel if your child always asks your neighbor for food, when you have a refrigerator full of food?

That's how God feels you should always come to him when you need something. One word from God can change your entire life.

You can't serve God and money at the same time, but you can serve God with your money. If you seek money without God, you will not keep it, but if you seek God, you will have money. God is always your source.

Sometimes your assignment is your job. God has you around people to show the world that he exists.

God can turn every wrong decision that you have made around. He will not let you remain in your mess.

Do Not Worry

Worry stops you from where you are going.
It comes when you are thinking too much about your future
instead of being thankful for what you have today.

God says, "If you focus on what I told you to do, I will focus on
what you asked me to do."

God said you will have challenges, but do not be so focused on
what is wrong that you miss what is right in your life.

Look at what is going good in your life right now, focus on
what you do have today!

I know one thing you do have today, and that's LIFE, as you
are reading this right now! The ability to see!

So be thankful for what you do have, because there is
someone that wishes they had what you have!

Never take today for granted!

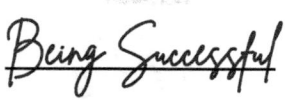

Being Successful

Sometimes when you're moving forward God may slow you down but not expect for you to get stuck in what he's trying to show you.

You're expected to make it through and be able to strengthen someone else that is encountering a storm that you have just gone through.

God wants you to stay humble, release your ego, and pray. It is hard for you to fall or get angry if you're praying.

Don't allow the past to disrupt your future and destroy your life. It's time to move on.

After your experience, you'll have wisdom to remember what God has done for you in the past. This will help you get through your hard days.

In all situations, know that God has a plan. Speak what you want to happen. Know that if God did It for someone else, he will definitely do it for you.

Don't be jealous, be thankful. God hears you every time you pray. Learn to open up your mouth and declare what you want to happen in your life.

Speaking Over Your Life

God has called everyone to be able to speak things into existence.

Speak what you want over your life. Do not insult God with doubtful thinking, or having low self-esteem that cause you to lose sight of what God has for you.

Speak boldly. Speak proudly to your mountain! Say "mountain be removed" and do not doubt in your heart and believe it will be done, then you will have what you say, whatever you are believing for.

Whatever you ask when you pray, believe that you will receive it, and you will have it.
It is okay to not know how things are going to happen, but speak it anyway!

If your heart is filled with God, your mouth will speak it, and you will have what you speak. If you believe what you're praying for you will have it. Don't start out in faith and then quit.

God will cause someone to step up and be a blessing to you and help you, keep doing God's will if you want God to do good to you.

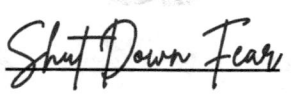

Shut Down Fear

It is important to pray continuously. Having faith is what moves God. He is always looking for our faith.

Faith mixed with what God's has told you will produce a beautiful outcome in your life every single time.

Don't allow your faith to be stopped by the spirit of fear.
Stop living by fear.
Start filling yourself up.

You're like an empty pot beginning to fill, from the bottom up.

- ❖ Starting with your feet that God is leading the way.
- ❖ Then go to your hands, so you can touch others with how God has taken care of you.
- ❖ Then to your heart, so you can show God's love to others.
- ❖ Then to your mouth, so you can speak truth.
- ❖ Then to your ears, so you can hear God.
- ❖ Then to your eyes, so you can see God's vision for you.
- ❖ Then to your head, so you can think like God until you overflow.

Big Faith

God will supply your every need.

Do not quit or give up. Stay on your faith.
It might not have happened yet but say it will happen.
If God has blessed you before, God will bless you again.

Believe what God says and keep saying it until it manifests.
A seed never looks like what it is going to become.
The seed you sow does not look like what you're going to receive from it.

When God tells you something to do, do it.
You can always count how many seeds are in a fruit, but you can never count the fruit in the seed.
The process of the seed takes time, it doesn't happen overnight.

When you're a blessing to others you're really a blessing to yourself.

If you don't quit, you will have what you're in faith for.

Thank You God

- ❖ Today I thank you God for a great day.
- ❖ Today I ask for forgiveness for my past and any negative energy be released from my heart.
- ❖ Today I thank you for a healthy body.
- ❖ Today I thank you for unexpected miracles happening to me.
- ❖ Today I thank you for a long happy life.
- ❖ Today I thank you for the ability to make money and enjoy what I do.
- ❖ Today I thank you for my happiness and my life is full of joy.
- ❖ Today I thank you for my life aligning into the way you want it to be.
- ❖ Today I thank you that my heart and spirit is full of love, it is healed, and it is at peace.
- ❖ Today I thank you for protecting me from any negativity.
- ❖ Today I thank you for the knowledge of knowing that what a person does has nothing to do with me and I do not take things personal anymore.
- ❖ Today I thank you for the strength to forgive those who have wronged me, and I choose to love them anyway.
- ❖ Today I thank you for fighting my battles.
- ❖ Today I thank you for allowing me to be a blessing to someone with my gifts.
- ❖ Today I thank you for a loving relationship.
- ❖ Today I thank you that my mind and spirit is at peace.

- ❖ Today I thank you that I do not feel lonely, and I feel loved.
- ❖ Today I thank you that all things are working for my good.
- ❖ Today I thank you that everything is working out better than I dreamed of.
- ❖ Today I thank you that I am surrounded by the right people.
- ❖ Today I simply thank you for your grace over my life.

Believe these things and more, even if they haven't happened yet.

Be specific with what you are believing in God for.

Your Manifestation List

Today, take the time to write down what you want the most to happen in your life. Read your list aloud every day for 30 days and check off the list as each thing manifest into your life.

☐ _____

☐ _____

☐ _____

☐ _____

☐ _____

☐ _____

☐ _____

☐ _____

☐ _____

☐ _____

Your Personal Affirmation List

What is an affirmation? It is a strategy used for you to believe in your own ability to do something and apply it into your life. Take the time to tell yourself 7 things that you will do this year and read it daily to keep yourself encouraged and accountable!

1.

_____

2.

_____

3.

_____

4.

_____

5.

_____

6.

_____

7.

_____

Your Thoughts

INSPIRATION REFERENCES

Important principles for a positive day.
The Four Agreements: A practical guide to personal freedom.
1997. Don Miguel Ruiz.

Attachments.
How attachment styles affect adult relationships.
HelpGuide.org. March 22, 2023. Lawrence Robinson, Jeanne
Segal, Ph.D. and Jaelline Jaffe, Ph.D.

Affirmation Definition.
How to make self-affirmation work, based on science.
Washingtonpost.com. May 2, 2023. Allyson Chiu